Stay strong &
keep the faith!

melissa

THE
QUEEN'S
DAUGHTER

She survived a woman's
worst nightmare.

A true story.

Melissa McCormick

WalkervillePublishing

Windsor, Ontario
Canada

Walkerville Publishing

201- 420 Devonshire Road
Windsor, Ontario
N9A 5N2 Canada
www.walkerville.com

Design and layout, including cover by Walkerville Publishing

Printed in China

ISBN
978-0-9784408-2-4

Some last names have been withheld to protect the privacy
of the individuals in question.

This book is
dedicated to the memory of
Mr. Walton Lewis –
a true philanthropist and humanitarian,
who devoted his life to elevating
society's perception of the black man.

Acknowledgments

I would like to thank God for allowing me to live this incredible life.

I would like to thank my parents for teaching me the value of faith, hard work and perseverance.

I would like to thank my three beautiful children who inspire me to be the best that I can be.

I am truly blessed to have a huge network of friends who have supported and helped me over the years - thank you all!

And last but not least – thank you to my best friend in the whole world – my sister Zorka. Without her endless love and support, I wouldn't have been able to survive this experience and become the woman I am today.

Contents

A Note from the Editor

Melissa and I met while attending grade school in Windsor, Ontario. As the years went by our lives followed different paths; by the time I had moved to Toronto to attend university, we were no longer in touch.

It was during my second year away that Melissa was assaulted. When details of what happened to her that February night in Detroit reached me, I was shocked to my core, especially when I heard that she had begged assailants to kill her.

I wondered how could anyone possibly have survived something that horrendous. I sincerely doubted that Melissa could ever live a normal life again.

When I next encountered Melissa, it was over twenty years later. She was a member of a women's business group I had joined after returning to Windsor. I was pleased to see her and relieved to learn that not only was she a successful business owner, she was also the mother of three children. She appeared extremely happy and well adjusted, with a ready laugh.

We became reacquainted and a few years later, Melissa approached me about a project. When she explained that she wanted my company, Walkerville Publishing, to help her produce the book she was writing about her ordeal, I was both surprised she had decided to pursue self-publishing and honored to assist her.

In the years following her life-altering experience, several publishers and magazines had contacted Melissa hoping to convince her to let them publish her story, but she had not been ready. She had so much to do simply to get her life back on track.

Many years later, Melissa felt stronger, and began working with a mass-market publisher. She did not like the direction they proposed to take with the book so she abandoned the project until the end of 2002, when she approached me.

Working with Melissa has been an incredible journey. It took considerable courage for her to write this book and to see this story finally in print. I am completely in awe of this woman.

It was evident that the writing and publishing process was extremely difficult for her. During our meetings and phone calls over the course of a year that this project has evolved, I helped

Melissa remember details and events from that terrible time as well as the intervening years, in order to fill in some of the gaps apparent in her original draft.

I knew it was difficult and painful for her to dwell on those years but I also appreciated that she did not want to write a book that sensationalized what had happened to her. I gently urged her to include some of the missing details as they were important for readers to properly understand not only what had happened to Melissa, but how she had summoned the strength to survive and overcome what is without a doubt, a woman's worst nightmare.

I think the final product tells her story as Melissa envisioned it and I'm proud to have helped her achieve this goal.

While this may not be an easy book to read, ultimately, I hope you find Melissa's story as inspiring as I do.

Elaine Weeks
Editor
Walkerville Publishing

Foreword

Never doubt that a small group of thoughtful committed citizens can change the world. Indeed, it is the only thing that ever has."

Margaret Mead

This is not a book for the faint of heart. Between these pages are the intimate details of what happened the night of February 12, 1976 on a dark, unpatrolled, Detroit freeway. This is the story of Melissa McCormick, an incredible woman, possessed of strength and dignity. She stills cares about how her experience, and its telling, will affect the lives of others. You will find yourself touched by her story, and above all else, you will like Melissa as you take the journey with her, the night she became, **The Queen's Daughter.**

The 1970s were a time when women began to believe that rape and violence against women, were not acceptable. It was our position that these were crimes motivated by the will to dominate, not enticement to sexual gratification. We needed to persuade the rest of the world that this was so. It was a huge leap sociologically. But we were ready for it. Rape Crisis Centers sprang up all over North America. Women were beginning to feel empowered. But through it all, there were time warps into which women continued to fall. And immense cracks in the justice system.

As a criminal lawyer and prosecutor in Windsor, and one of the founding members of SACC (Sexual Assault Crisis Centre of Essex County) in the 70's, I was aware of Melissa's ordeal. We all were. It was a shocking and frightening thing to hear the details of what had happened to her. It was the topic of discussion at water coolers all over Windsor. It caused a collective shudder in the hearts and minds of women in the community. Our professional knowledge aside, we were first and foremost women, and, when we read Melissa's story in the newspapers, we reacted, not as lawyers and prosecutors, but as women.

There were no cellular phones then. If we were unlucky enough to have a flat tire on the side of a Detroit freeway, we had to rely on the kindness of strangers. We drove to Joe Muer's and other fine dining establishments and bars in Detroit, on a regular basis. We were often unaccompanied by men. This could so easily have happened to any of us. Melissa *was* "us."

However in 1976, (and even, shockingly, sometimes today) the commonly held belief and myth was that rape was primarily a "sexual" act. Persons with this belief unintentionally (or, some would argue, intentionally) placed the victim on trial. Her motives, her dress and her actions became suspect not only to law enforcement officials but also to her family and friends. The woman's credibility may have been questioned, and her sexual activity and private life may have been made public.

Perhaps because of the guilt, embarrassment and humiliation, rape has traditionally been a highly underreported crime.

However, throughout the past 30 years a variety of psychologists and sociologists have studied the psychology of rape and rapists. In reviewing the research of the day, the findings demonstrated, to the surprise of many, that rape was a crime of violence, often regarded by the woman as a life-threatening act, in which fear and humiliation were her dominant emotions.

It began to be understood that *sexual desire* was less a motivation for the man than *violent aggression*. Shockingly, it was found that approximately 71% of rapes were planned. The choice of victim was often left to chance and circumstance, but the rapist set out to rape someone. Planning was even more prevalent in pair or gang rapes. (Amir, Menachem, *Patterns in Forcible Rape*, Chicago: University of Chicago Press, 1971).

The National Institute of Law Enforcement and Criminal Justice examined the characteristics and behaviors of rapists in five cities during the mid 1980s: Seattle, Detroit, Kansas City, New Orleans and Phoenix. There were several similarities between their findings and Menachem Amir's. Both found minority males were over-represented; that most victims tended to be under 30 years old; and most rapists did some planning before the rape occurred. The use of weapons varied from city to city, but it was found that they were used in approximately half the assaults (Horos, Carol, *Rape*. Toby Publishing Co., New Canaan, CT, 1974. p. 21).

Offenders interviewed by members of the National Institute

at a maximum security state mental hospital believed that the prevention or avoidance of rape was the responsibility of the women. Their advice, typically sexist, advised women not to go out alone, not to hitchhike, not to drink alone and to learn self-defense. A widely accepted theory was that most rapists came from a subculture of violence whose values may be different from those of the dominant culture. Therefore these adolescents and young men were demonstrating their toughness and masculinity in a more violent and antisocial manner. (Brownmiller, Susan. *Against Our Will: Men, Women and Rape*. New York, Simon and Schuster, 1975, p. 183)

This research was conducted in the 70's. Have we really come such a long way, baby?

I write this in 2004. We now know that violence against women involves the use of force or the threat of the use of force. The most recent federal statistics tell us that sexual assault is still very pervasive in Canada. Fifty-one per cent of all Canadian women have experienced at least one incident of sexual or physical violence. Close to 60% of these women have survived more than one incident of violence (*Statistics Canada* 1993).

Recent statistics still list Detroit as one of the most violent cities in North America, despite attempts by local politicians to eradicate its violent image. These attempts have been an abysmal failure. The FBI Uniform Crime Reports released in November 2002 indicate that Detroit still has 22,112 violent crimes annually of which 811 are categorized as "rapes."

Detroit has an average of 83 rapes per 100,000 population,

as compared to the national average of 30.

There are many difficult passages in this book. The hardest for me to read was the quote from an unknown woman, allegedly commenting on Melissa's ordeal by saying: "being raped by black men is actually a sexual fantasy for most white women."

Really?

I cannot imagine a more profound misunderstanding of the female psyche. This was a horrific act of violence and torture, the type that occurs in developing countries involved in civil war. It should never have happened in a "civilized society." It should never have happened at all.

Melissa was determined not to let her feelings of shame, humiliation and pain overshadow her need to hold these men accountable for their actions and to do her part to ensure that other women would not fall prey to their violence. As a result of her determination and bravery, the freeways of Detroit City are still patrolled by state police. This is her legacy.

Melissa's story will inspire you. It will make you want to know her better. It will surely lead you to conclude that change occurs in tiny steps, by those who care. Not in large leaps, by politicians or the wealthy. This book is a labor of love, produced and published by women. It's a keeper, for sure.

Paulah Dauns
Adjudicator

Preface

In 1989, I received a call from Dr. Claude Vincent, a sociology professor at the University of Windsor, who explained that he was conducting research for a new book about victims of crime. The purpose of the book was to reveal how these people's lives had progressed after ten years.

My kidnapping and brutal sexual assault in Detroit was a highly publicized story in 1976. Apparently, Dr. Vincent had documented the news information from the onset.

His book would eventually be used as a textbook for sociology students at the university and not for public exposure. This criterion was extremely important in my decision to co-operate, for over the years I had felt exploited during interviews by reporters, magazine writers, journalists and the media who often contacted me for my story. Their motivations were insincere. I would only conduct an interview if it could ultimately help someone else.

Dr. Vincent assured me that indeed this project's outcome would help the education process and that my contribution would be an interesting addition to his research. Dr. Vincent's request for an interview seemed genuine so I agreed to meet with him in his office at the university.

During the hour-long interview, Dr. Vincent never once asked me about the crime itself. His focus was on my present daily lifestyle and routine. He questioned me about my work, my family, my marriage and my friends. He was interested in my life goals and my values, my hobbies and what I did for fun.

Time passed quickly and soon the meeting was over, but before leaving Dr. Vincent told me, "Melissa, I have interviewed over ten other people who suffered as victims in various ways; a woman who lost her daughter to a drunk driver; a boy who was set on fire by his stepfather; and a woman molested by a relative as a child. The crimes committed against you are by far worse than any I have researched, yet after meeting and talking with you this hour, I realize that in comparison to the others, your life is the most normal. You seem to be handling everything much better than anyone would expect under the circumstances.

You should consider sharing your ordeal with others to help those in similar situations because there is something unique about you. Maybe you should be writing a book."

I was honored that Dr. Vincent viewed my experience as an example for helping others and I agreed that I would write my story some day, not to sensationalize it, or to exploit the situation, but to tell it in the hope that it will touch someone.

It was several more years after my meeting with Dr. Vincent before I decided to finally tell my story. My decision was based on my belief that people need to know that rape should not be a "taboo" subject and that rape victims should not be treated like pariahs. Rather than be swept under the carpet, the crime of rape should be discussed with the victim and the victim should be encouraged to open up and release the pent-up anger, fear, isolation and humiliation that is felt after such a violation of the self.

Rape victims are seldom treated with the understanding and empathy that they desperately need. They are often treated as the perpetrator rather than the one who is being violated. Frequently, rape victims are the ones being put on trial rather than the other way around.

I also want people to know that like every other rape victim, I deserve the respect that I earned fighting for my life.

Melissa McCormick

THE
QUEEN'S
DAUGHTER

Freedom

Friday the thirteenth. The time of day is unknown. I sit, waiting. I cannot move. My eyes slowly survey the room and again I see the picture of the Isley Brothers. I remember hearing earlier, "A black man from the ghetto can only make it two ways – sports or rock music."

I sit on the couch that occupies half of the room, a bedroom converted to a den. My back is toward the door that leads to a narrow hall.

Joe enters the den and crouches to look at my swollen face. For a moment, I sense what might be compassion in his eyes or in his voice.

"Mark and the other guys will be here soon with your car and then you can go home," he says. He makes an effort to sound reassuring, but promises of freedom don't register anymore.

Although Joe is not a big man, he projects power. He stands around five foot ten and is quite thin except for the muscles that are visible only when he is naked. His skin is medium black and his hair is styled in a short Afro. His profile is mean, his face haunting and mysterious. Among his friends he is the undisputed leader.

Joe is violent, angry at the world, and as much as I hate him, I also pity him.

He leaves the room and again I am left alone to sit and wait. Suddenly I hear angry voices. The tension is high.

"No way, man!" yells someone. "We let her go and she'll run to the cops. She can identify us, man!"

"Ya! I say we kill her like we planned."

"Ya, we can dump the body in the ditch at the end of the street," says another.

Then I recognize Joe's voice: "I say we let her go."

Suddenly he is standing beside me. "Follow me and just do what I tell you," he commands. He holds me tightly by the upper arm, and we go out the front door of the house.

The sun hurts my eyes. I squint. To my left I see five of the men from the night before.

I look to Joe for direction. He glares at me and orders in a clear, dominating voice, "Get in the car and drive."

My yellow Pacer, now somewhat damaged, is parked on the street and the driver's side door is wide open. I do not hesitate for I know that when Joe gives an order, you obey.

One of the five men explains, "To get to the tunnel back to Canada, drive down there." He points to the end of the street, but I remember the ditch they talked of earlier. I get in the car and drive in the opposite direction.

My movements are mechanical since I am still in shock from

the previous night. There is a stoplight ahead indicating a busy intersection. I think about how to leave Detroit and get back to Windsor without drawing attention to myself.

I just want to go home to my tiny apartment and my regular routine and pretend that nothing happened.

But my wallet had been stolen leaving me without money for the tunnel passage or identification to get back into Canada.

After driving two blocks, I notice a police cruiser parked on the right side of the street. A policeman is sitting behind the wheel writing a report. I park behind his cruiser and as I get out of my car, I can feel that I am actually alive. For the first time in over twelve hours, my movement to approach the policeman is of my own choice.

My intent is simply to ask for directions but the moment the officer looks at me, I break down and sob hysterically, my body shaking with fright.

"Help me please! They are following me! They're going to kill me!" I plead.

"Nobody is going to hurt you. Calm down," he assures me.

He helps me into the back seat of the police car and soon there are more policemen present.

"I'm Sergeant Lennon," the first police officer says. "Tell me, *who* is going to hurt you?" He is a husky man with an authoritative presence.

"The men who kidnapped me last night – they are following me!"

"Tell me exactly what happened."

"I was raped."

"How many men are you talking about?"

"There were about ten or twelve."

"Which one of them raped you? Can you remember his name?

I cry uncontrollably, punching my fists into the air. I scream, "They all did! They all took turns raping me!"

This outburst leaves me emotionally and physically exhausted. I begin rocking myself back and forth, wishing I were dead.

The Sergeant is visibly upset and his obvious display of anger alleviates part of my burden. After many assurances of my safety, we proceeded to cruise the streets in the area hoping to locate the house from which I had just left, but a positive identification is impossible.

Eventually I am taken to the Sexual Assault Unit at the Detroit police station where information is needed about the rape.

I just want to go home, to be alone and forget, perhaps start all over. I want to wake up from this horrible nightmare.

But before I can go back to Canada, I have to tell the police my story.

Independence

In 1974, I had graduated with honors from Walkerville Collegiate Institute in Windsor, Ontario, Canada, located directly south of the big city of Detroit, Michigan. I played the violin in the school orchestra, was a member of the United Nations Club, and the student council. My life goals revolved around attaining freedom and independence. I wanted to work to have my own apartment and car. I wanted to travel, live life to the fullest, and create memories.

I did not want regret to be a part of my vocabulary when I looked back on my life.

This would prove to be a challenge because I had been brought up in a very strict Serbian Orthodox home. We attended church every Sunday and I sang in the choir. Our family's social life revolved around the Serbian community and the continuance of the culture. We spoke the language at home and observed the religious holidays.

My parents had taught my siblings, my sister, three brothers and me, to work hard and to value money. Being immigrants to Canada they had struggled to build a life for our family. We lived a frugal and unpretentious lifestyle that revolved around value and religion. As much as I respected what they had overcome to provide us with a decent life, I wanted more.

I knew that with perseverance and focus I could achieve all of my dreams and I looked forward to a promising future.

After I graduated from high school, I found a full-time job as a server in a local downtown nightclub called the Top Hat. It offered two nightly floorshows featuring up-and-coming singing stars and it had a house band for dancing.

I loved working at the Top Hat where I was surrounded by friends. My boss was a respected businessman who was also a member of the Serbian community. His name was Mike Drakich, and he was not only a second father to me but also a mentor. He treated me like a daughter and it was always understood that he hoped that someday I would marry one of his four sons.

Work and saving money were my focus and within a year, I could afford to move out of my parents' home and into my own place. Convincing my mom and dad to support my efforts at independence was another matter. I was told, "Good girls don't leave home until they get married."

But soon an opportunity presented itself that was ideal; a small apartment became available in a triplex that my parents owned as an income property. My older sister Zorka, her husband Jim, and my baby niece occupied half of the house; the other half was split into an upstairs and a downstairs apartment.

My parents finally agreed that if I was to move out, it was safer to live next door to my sister than in a strange apartment and neighborhood. At 19 years of age, I was thrilled to take this important step towards independence. I moved into one of the apartments a short time later.

Zorka and I have always had a very close relationship. Even though we are four years apart and our personalities are very different, (she is reserved and introspective while I am outgoing and open), we complement each other very well.

Growing up we shared the same bedroom and we kept very few secrets from each other. It was not unusual for us to discuss our current boyfriends, the latest fashion trends, problems at school and our parents' strict rules, for hours on end. We were each other's confidants and we helped each other sort out our various teenage dilemmas.

When Zorka got married, I was her maid of honor and we continued our close relationship. I even gained a good friend in her new husband Jim. We enjoyed many laughs and good times together. Zorka and Jim were both supportive of me in my life, as I was of them in theirs.

I enjoyed popping over to their place regularly, to sip tea and chat about current events, the latest gossip and whatever was going on in our own lives.

My adorable little niece Charlotte was a continuous source of amusement and it was a pleasure to watch her grow and develop right before my eyes.

Those were good times and I cherished those moments. Unbeknownst to any of us, one of the biggest bombshells of our lives was about to explode into our relatively uncomplicated world.

Every day when I took the bus to work from my new home, I would pass by an American Motors car lot where I would see on display their latest model, the "Pacer," a compact, futuristic-looking bubble-shaped car.

I loved that car.

My next goal became to buy a Pacer, a bright yellow one – my favorite color, because it reminded me of the sun.

After saving for a down payment and, with my father's signature, I soon obtained a car loan and became the proud owner of my very own bright yellow Pacer. I was well on my way to becoming an independent woman with my own cute little apartment, and now a new car.

Living in Windsor was fine for its smaller city attractions, but because it was situated right across the river from Detroit, we could also enjoy big city offerings. Canadians love hockey and Windsorites especially loved the Detroit Red Wings. We also loved Motown music and frequenting Detroit's fabulous restaurants and nightclubs.

Unfortunately, Detroit had another side, a much darker and more dangerous one. In 1967, riots between core area blacks and the police had drastically changed the city. Many Detroit residents fled to the suburbs because of increased crime and a skyrocketing murder rate.

But these facts didn't phase me. I loved Detroit! Its enterprising and industrial atmosphere mesmerized me. My sister and I would often take the tunnel bus over to the downtown shopping area, which back in the 1970's housed the famous Hudson's Department Store. Woodward Avenue, the main shopping strip, was always bustling with shoppers and office workers.

I remember feeling such excitement walking among the crowds of people on the streets. Sometimes as a joke, I would pretend I was Marlo Thomas, from the TV show "That Girl," and I would throw my hat in the air and mess up my hair just like she did at the beginning of every show.

My schedule at the Top Hat was full. I worked every lunch from noon to 2p.m. and then I would return at 6p.m. and work until the dinner hour and floorshow were over. Thursday night was the only evening I had free to go out and socialize with my friends.

A Night Out

On Thursday, February 12th, 1976, my friends and I looked forward to a night on the town. Nothing was happening in Windsor, but we knew something was always going on in Detroit. Now that was the happening place to party!

Annie and Vera, my co-workers at the Top Hat, Annie's roommate Anita, Vera's sister Rad and Rad's friend Diane and I got ready to take on the town. We were six young and beautiful women looking for a big night out.

We crossed the tunnel to Detroit in two cars. Diane, Rad and Vera rode with me while the other two girls went in the other car. While we were careful to lock our car doors after we passed through customs, we weren't overly concerned for our safety.

We chose to have an elegant dinner at a seafood restaurant called Joe Muer's, which catered to Detroit's elite. It was common to see a celebrity or a politician dining discreetly , and to hear the whispers of the patrons discussing who's who.

Of course we had dressed for the occasion and we all looked fabulous. Heads turned when we were led to our table.

My looks were very Eastern European. I was very slim and my long hair was dark brown, as were my eyes. That night I wore a black polka dotted two-piece pantsuit. The top was low cut with long puffy sleeves and shoulders, and it had a wrap-around sash that tied at the back. My pants were tight around the waist and behind and they ballooned from the thigh to below the knee where they tucked into my black leather four-inch heeled boots. I accessorized with a gold choker with a black medallion.

I looked like a Russian Cossack and I was stunning. My outfit was completed with a full-length pure white rabbit fur coat, which accented my dark features.

Our dinner was incredibly good and afterwards we sat enjoying the atmosphere and good conversation.

Rad and Diane had planned to meet friends at a Southfield disco called "The Landing." I was hesitant to drive to an unfamiliar area outside of Detroit but my friends reassured me that it would be worth the trip and that we'd have a good time, so off we went.

When we arrived at the disco I was immediately struck by the fascinating decor, which was based on an airplane theme: the bucket seats were like those in a real plane and the bar was built like a cockpit. The bartenders were all dressed like pilots and the waitresses looked like flight attendants.

Even though the place was jammed with people and the room was thick with smoke, we were conspicuously the only white people in the room.

The cold stares from the female patrons were intimidating and made me uneasy. The men were whistling and shouting, "Ooooh baby!" Offers of drinks for us were already forthcoming.

Annie and Anita announced, "Hey, this isn't our scene. Let's get out of here." Considering how uncomfortable I felt as well, I quickly agreed. Meanwhile, the other three girls, Vera, Rad and Diane, wanted to stay and wait for their friends.

At around 11p.m., the three of us left in two separate cars. Annie drove with Anita and I agreed to meet up with them again at the University of Windsor Pub.

I followed them alone in my car.

Flat Tire

As we drove back I could see Anita's car just ahead on the John Lodge Freeway. We were only ten minutes away from the tunnel back to Windsor.

Suddenly I felt a twinge of premonition that something was wrong. A split second later I was shocked to hear my tire blow. Traffic was heavy and speeds were high but I managed to move to the right of the highway where I stopped my car with my four-way lights flashing. I really hoped that my friends had seen me slow down and come to a stop.

I was afraid to pull onto the freeway shoulder, so instead I stayed in the right lane. I got out of the car so that someone would see I was in trouble. Minutes later a car pulled up behind me. A man, whose name I later learned was Freddy Bennett, stuck his head out of his car window and asked, "What's the matter lady?"

"I have a flat tire!" I answered.

"Well, pull over to the side and I'll help you change it!" he yelled back.

I gratefully drove my car onto the shoulder of the highway as he pulled up behind me. He then proceeded to change the tire.

Freddy was a tall, young black man with a slim build. His voice was friendly and he had a Michigan accent. To me, he was truly a Good Samaritan. I kept thanking him as he worked, while in the back of my mind I tried to remember how much money I had left in my wallet. I wanted to pay him for taking the trouble to stop and help me.

Just as Freddy was putting away the jack and the ruined tire, I noticed a couple of vehicles stopping a little ahead of my Pacer. A group of black men got out of a black Cadillac and started walking toward us, talking and laughing in a casual way. As they approached, one of them asked, "Hey, you need any help?"

I was standing at the left side of the car and I instinctively moved toward Freddy who was still standing behind it.

The closer these men advanced, the more afraid I became. Something was suspiciously shady.

Within seconds we were surrounded. The men were inches away from me and I could feel a jab at my side. When I looked down to see what it was, I saw a gun!

"This is a stick up bitch – take off the coat!"

They stripped the coat off of my trembling body, and then took my jewelry.

Next they shoved me toward the front of the car and one of them said, "We want the keys and your wallet."

My purse was in the front seat and as I reached in to pick it up, it was snatched away by one of the men.

There was commotion at the rear of the Pacer and I heard Freddy say, "Come on man, you don't want to do this."

"Shut up nigger!" was the response.

The men forced me to walk toward the black Cadillac.

A man was on each side of me holding me firmly under the arms.

"Oh my God," I thought. "They're taking me with them!"

They led me to the car and as they guided me into the back seat I made a desperate effort to get free. I kicked the man behind me as hard as I could and I ran toward the freeway. He chased after me and, in his attempt to stop me, he grabbed the sash at the back of my blouse, untying it and exposing my white bra.

I ran frantically into the right lane of the freeway screaming desperately for someone to stop and help me, my blouse flying open in the cold wind. Cars swerved to avoid me, but no one stopped.

Then I heard, "You mother fuckin' white bitch!" Someone punched me in the face and I blacked out.

When I regained consciousness I found myself in the front seat of a moving car. I was sitting between two men. My bra was undone, my breasts exposed and hands were all over me; hands from the back seat and the front seat.

My thoughts were scrambled with disbelief; could this really be happening to me or, was I in the middle of a bad dream?

I pretended to be still unconscious. I could hear the men debating where to take me. Somebody's mother wasn't home so we were going to his place. I concluded that there were four men in the back seat and two in the front. My Pacer pulled up beside us on the highway and I could see two more men.

(I later learned that while I was being kidnapped, Freddy was being tied up and stuffed into the hatchback of the Pacer. He was later pushed out of the vehicle, while it continued down the freeway. Eventually, he managed to untie himself and make it back to his own car. After he drove home, he reported everything to the police.)

Within minutes we were traveling through a run-down residential neighborhood. It was very dark, shadowy and unfamiliar. By now the men must have realized that I was conscious but they talked around me and not to me.

As the car came to a stop somewhere, one of them said, "Tie up her blouse to cover her and put on these sunglasses so she can't see anything."

With hands all over me again, and the sunglasses on, I was dragged out of the car and escorted up some steep steel stairs at the back of an apartment building. By now one of my boots had lost its four-inch heel, probably as a result of my trying to escape on the freeway. I wobbled into a small apartment. The glasses came off and I was pushed into a back bedroom.

I fell onto a bed as the men pulled and ripped at my clothes until I was completely naked.

Go Ahead: Kill Me!

Everything was happening so quickly. Terrified, I lay on my back on the bed feeling the cold gun at my temple while the men argued who would go first. Who would have the privilege of raping me first?

They were like a pack of wolves ready to devour their prey.

"Please God, let me wake up from this horrible nightmare!" I prayed.

Then each man took his turn shoving his penis into me.

I had never experienced such pain in my life. I could smell their bodies and hear them panting as they forced themselves on me.

I couldn't turn away, fearing the gun that was constantly pointed at my temple. I was at their mercy and I felt death was looming.

At one point one of them dangled his penis over my face and demanded that I put it in my mouth but another one, who appeared to be the gang leader, announced, "She don't have to do that shit – she's the Queen's daughter."

Apparently the only thing my assailants knew about Canada

was that it had a reigning Queen, therefore I was probably the Queen's daughter. I believe that the presumption that I was royalty saved me from having to perform oral sex and God knows what else. Throughout the rest of my ordeal, I was referred to as *"The Queen's Daughter."*

As they continued the invasion of my body, not only was I in excruciating pain, but I also became overwhelmed with feelings of shame and embarrassment. I was being exposed to the greatest humiliation possible. I started losing my soul because of the degrading abuse that I was being subjected to, and then I completely lost myself.

Suddenly I experienced something so profound that I can still recall it today; I had an out-of-body experience. My body and my spirit separated and I was now on the outside looking in.

A tremendous feeling of peace overtook my entire being. I knew at that moment that I was indeed going to die. My life flashed before my eyes and I could see my parents, my brothers and my sister, her husband and my baby niece Charlotte.

Her cute little face and smile always brought me such happiness.

I thanked God for the good life that I had lived up to this point and I embraced death with complete acceptance.

"I am ready God," I surrendered. "Please take me now."

Suddenly I was jolted back to reality by a command that I hadn't quite grasped because I had resigned myself to death.

With yet another threat of continued harm if I didn't do what I was told, I cried out for the first time and screamed,

"Go ahead: kill me, shoot that fucking gun! Kill me, damn it!"

I started to sob. "I want to die! Please kill me, please!"

I was now sitting upright on the bed, crying uncontrollably. I again begged the man with the gun to kill me.

From the corner of the room the gang leader realized that my outburst was causing him to lose control over the situation. His anger became all encompassing, and when I looked in his direction I became so frightened that I couldn't catch my breath.

He charged at me with incredible speed and kicked me hard in the chest. I fell back on the bed with him on top of me, his hands fiercely gripping my neck.

His grip was so strong and powerful that my body immediately felt limp and weak in his hold. I could see pure evil in his black piercing eyes.

"You die when I say you die bitch. I'll kill you. I do the killing!"

He kept choking as I frantically gasped for air. Eventually, the other guys pulled him off of me saying, "You can't kill her here! The nigger's mother is coming home!" Some tried to calm him down while two of them escorted me into the bathroom.

One of them handed me a wet rag to wash the blood from my thighs, my vaginal area and my stomach. They allowed me to use the toilet and as I urinated they conversed with me as if my presence was voluntary.

They commented on how pretty I was and that my figure was perfect – not too skinny. "Brothers don't like skinny," they agreed.

Meanwhile my head was spinning with horror and confusion,

my body overcome with pain. "What the hell is going on?" I thought. 'Why are these guys talking to me and why am I not dead? I should be dead!'

By now my reactions had become automatic. I did what I was told as a gun was always visible to remind me of my inevitable death.

My mind became numb from pain and abuse, and I could take no more. I went into a state of shock.

All of a sudden there was a bang on the door and the leader's voice demanded entrance into the bathroom. Apparently he felt it imperative to re-establish the fact that he was running this show.

The two men left and the man who was strangling me just minutes ago, barged in. Clever Joe, (as he was referred to by the others), and I were alone. He already had the respect of the other guys but he still needed to assert his leadership by claiming me as his own.

"You will be my slave and my whore," he declared. "You only have sex when I say so. You have sex with who I say you have sex with."

With this pronouncement he laid claim to his territory.

He instructed me to lean over the bathtub. I obeyed and he raped me again and again with a vengeance.

When he was finally satisfied I discovered I was no longer in pain. I had totally lost myself. Although my body was alive, my spirit was dead. I could neither feel nor think; I was merely going through the motions.

These animals had reduced me to an animal too. The person I once was, was gone forever.

Dance, Queen's Daughter, Dance!

How I had moved from the bathroom into the living room I do not know, but suddenly I was there with all of the men. Somehow I was dressed, minus my bra and underwear and was standing in the middle of the room. Loud music was playing and the men were drinking and smoking. It was like a party, with me, as the guest of honor.

The room was spinning and everything was hazy.

"Dance, Queen's Daughter, dance!" the men yelled.

Although I didn't realize it at the time, due to my shock and the confused state of my mind, it was at this moment that the first shot was fired. The men were trying to scare me into dancing and when I didn't cooperate a second shot was fired, this time aimed to kill. Incredibly, the guy missed!

The next thing I remember was sitting on a sofa with voices talking at me. I had no idea what they were saying so I just nodded yes. There was mention of a guy named Bernard who wanted my car to take to school the next day. He asked me if I had finished high school.

"Yes," I answered softly.

Bernard was physically the smallest of my assailants. He was short, very young-looking and earlier during the rape, when the men were arguing about who would go next, I had pointed to him because I remembered his penis being so small that it was the only penetration that wasn't excruciatingly painful.

"I'm going to finish school too so that I can get a good job," he said nonchalantly.

The other men teased him about his comment, laughing, "Nigger, you ain't gonna finish no school!"

I pondered their use of that "N" word. Repeatedly hearing them call each other nigger was confusing. I was taught never to use that racist word under any circumstances because it depicted a black man in a very derogatory way. So why were they calling each other that name?

Another new expression that I heard that night was "mother fucker." Of course I knew the word "fuck" but never with the word "mother" in front of it. I found the expression totally vulgar and offensive.

"Yes, you should go to school Bernard," I thought. "Because anyone who thinks I am the 'Queen's Daughter' is totally clueless."

At about 1 or 2am, it was time to leave the apartment because someone's mother was coming home; so Clever Joe told one of the guys to drive him and me to Dell's house to get some drugs. They gave me an old plaid coat to wear along with the sunglasses from before. Joe led me out of the apartment and into another car.

I didn't know where or how long we drove but it occurred to me that being taken to another location meant certain death. It didn't matter though, because I would rather be dead than let Clever Joe pass me around to his friends.

In my heart, I already was dead.

The Test

Dell lived in a small bungalow in what appeared to be a much better neighborhood than the one of my previous captivity. Joe and I entered a small living room, plainly decorated but very clean and uncluttered. As Clever Joe and Dell exchanged handshakes and verbal greetings, it was obvious that Joe really wanted to make a good impression.

He introduced me as his "woman."

Dell was a clean-cut black man with short hair, a boyish face and quiet demeanor. He asked us to sit and offered us a drink. I looked to Joe for direction and he accepted for both of us. While Dell was in the kitchen, Joe sat next to me on the sofa and pulled out a small gun from his pocket.

"Have you ever shot a gun before?" he asked me.

I shook my head no. Carrying handguns was illegal in Canada.

It was a small silver pistol that fit in the palm of his hand and Joe proceeded to demonstrate how to load it and aim to shoot. He then gave me the gun and told me to hold onto it for safekeeping. The sheer boldness of this peculiar gesture suggested that he was somehow testing me. Was Joe trying to find out if he could trust me? Or, was he trying to connect with me in some strange way?

The gun remained in my pocket for an hour, the entire time the three of us were in the living room. Dell asked my name and where I was from. I answered, "Melissa, from Canada."

Even though I was an unkempt mess at this point, Dell appeared not to notice and acted as if I was here with Clever Joe of my own accord. He treated me like regular company visiting socially.

Dell lit a joint and shared it with Clever Joe, and when it was passed to me I shyly said, "No, thank you." I had never taken drugs in my life and I didn't want to start now. I later learned that Dell was actually a major drug dealer, which explained Joe's desire to impress him.

Joe then offered Dell a free night to sample my sexual services.

"Isn't she pretty? Wouldn't I make a good pimp for her?" Joe bragged.

Since he was my "pimp" and I was his "woman," Joe wanted Dell's opinion on how much he could charge his other friends for my services. Hearing this, I was horrified and instantly thought about the gun in my pocket.

I assessed the situation; there were two men against me and I couldn't be sure if the gun was really loaded. If I did escape where would I find myself? Detroit is a big city. I decided to go with my first instinct, the one that told me I was being tested.

If that was the case, it would be too risky to make any moves, so I continued to sit quietly.

When Joe asked for the gun, I reached into my pocket and when I gave it back to him I noticed a pleased look on his face. He needed to assert that he was completely in control and that he could trust that I would do as I was told.

As the men conversed, my eyelids became heavy and I began to slip away into a much-needed sleep, only to be startled abruptly by Joe's commanding voice.

"I want you to go to the bedroom with Dell."

Joe watched as we both undressed. I was so tired that I just wanted to sleep. I felt like a zombie lying in bed when I realized that Dell didn't seem overly interested.

Clever Joe excused himself from the room but I knew he was watching, because as Dell fumbled around trying to get an erection, Joe re-entered the room and uttered with frustration, "I'll show you how it's done!" He climbed on top of me and once again proceeded to plunge his penis into me.

I tried to avoid thinking of the horrific pain of his penetration and forced myself to think of other things, anything that would help me endure this latest invasion.

When Joe finished, he encouraged Dell to take his turn, but again he could not get an erection. My mind was so numb with this sequence of events that I could barely process what was taking place. The three of us finally fell asleep with me lying in between the two men.

A short time later I awoke freezing cold, lying naked in a pool of blood. As my mind registered everything that had happened, I reluctantly re-assessed my situation.

I was still alive!

I quickly reasoned that this might be the only chance I would have to save myself. At the same time, another part of me realized that if I did not succeed, I would have to resign myself to my fate.

How could I possibly get away?

Dell was not a threat (he was not violent), but Joe had the gun, which meant he still held the power.

I would somehow have to outsmart Joe.

"Yes," I thought, "I will play the game. To escape this living hell I will trick Joe into trusting me."

I slowly slid out of bed and tiptoed to the kitchen. I was incredibly thirsty and I needed a drink of water. I found a glass and as I drank, Joe's sudden appearance startled me. Again, I was overcome by fear.

"What are you doing?" he demanded.

"I'm sorry; I was thirsty," I answered in a soft, sweet voice as I lowered my eyes in submission. I slipped past him back into the bedroom and I returned to my spot beside the sleeping Dell. Joe appeared to be pleased with his undeniable control over me. He was the master; I was his woman.

A Way Out

The morning sun lit the den as I sat sideways on a small sofa. I was wearing my pantsuit and I had a blanket pulled up to my chin to keep me warm. One minute I wanted to die, the next minute I wanted to live.

In order for me to escape, my plan had to focus on Clever Joe. He would ultimately determine my fate, and he would be the key to my survival.

The two men were conversing in the next room. Dell wanted to know when we would be leaving. He was expecting someone to drop in to buy drugs and he wanted us out.

Joe entered the den and pulled up a chair to sit across from me. He stared at my face for what seemed like an eternity. I guessed that he was unsure of his next move. I knew that this was my chance to sway Joe. It was now or never. I had to convince him that I recognized some hints of civility behind that hard, cruel exterior.

When there was just the two of us, I was sure that I had sensed some compassion in his eyes or his voice. There had to be more to him than his depraved behavior indicated.

What would he do with me?

I lightly touched a scar on his bare chest.

"Where did you get this?" I asked him in a soft, concerned voice.

"I fought in Vietnam," he answered, and proudly proceeded to explain his many other scars. On his back were two bullet wounds from the war, as well as several knife marks on his arms and chest. Joe talked openly about Vietnam and how the experience had completely changed his life.

Although he did not want to go to Vietnam, he confessed that it was a good experience for him because it was there that he learned how to fight and where he really learned about death.

He expressed admiration for Richard Nixon; how he was a truly powerful President and he applauded the outcome of the Watergate scandal. He loved the fact that Nixon had gotten away with it and that this showed his real power.

I wanted to keep the conversation flowing, so I asked Joe about the framed picture on the desk.

"Those are the Isley Brothers. A black man from the ghetto can only make it two ways: sports or rock music."

It just so happened that I loved the Isley Brothers and I told him so. I had stumbled upon unexpected common ground, so I took a chance.

"You have to let me go soon," I told him nervously. "My family must be wondering where I am."

Joe stood up quickly, and in a rage, stomped out of the room, returning seconds later with something in his hand.

"Don't you fucking lie to me," he growled as he revealed my check book. He opened my check register, which showed my itemized expenses and he pointed out the line that read "Rent."

They didn't call him "Clever Joe" for nothing. He knew what I was up to and he wasn't falling for it. Uncharacteristically, however, the next decision he made would change *his* life forever.

I began to cry and said, "You're right! I live alone and nobody knows that I'm gone. But if I can get to work on time, nobody will know anything!"

I continued pleading: "I start work at noon today! I won't say anything, I promise! Please let me go home!"

It was abundantly clear that Joe's existence was all about power. I instinctively understood that aspect of his psyche and I had conducted myself accordingly. My survival instinct guided my reactions to his brutal commands.

When, for my own purposes, I took the time to relate to him as a human being, his demeanor changed and it was during these short moments that he softened toward me. He even suggested that it was too bad that we hadn't met under different circumstances. Considering we came from two different worlds, I found his remark unthinkable.

When I look back, I believe that in some bizarre way he had respect for me. I believe that I surprised him by not resisting and even being submissive when he was exerting his domination.

I showed Joe that I knew my place and recognized his power. It was during those moments that I both hated and felt pity for him. I felt sorry that he required violence and threats to make someone respond to him. I also hated him for what he was doing to me.

I believe that Clever Joe let me go that day because I had awakened in him a vulnerability that he thought no longer existed – his humanity. I don't know what life experiences had made him so hard and cruel, but I knew that I had to appeal to other aspects of his personality.

Joe went against everything he projected onto the surface when he let me go, but perhaps, deep down inside, he saw the pitiful person in front of him. Perhaps we understood each other in some bizarre, inexplicable manner.

Whatever the case, it was this dichotomy in Joe that saved my life.

At The Police Station

After driving away from Dell's place and encountering the police, I was taken to the police station. There I learned that Freddy Bennett, the man who had helped me change my tire, had reported my abduction and that a bulletin had been issued for my whereabouts. My disheveled appearance and yellow Pacer with Canadian license plates were a dead give-away as to my identity.

Accompanied by several policemen, I entered a floor of the Detroit Police Department that was allocated specifically for sexual assault cases.

It was an enormous, warehouse-type open space and I was amazed by the activity and commotion. I was seated next to a desk which belonged to Sergeant Barbara Weide. Although I felt completely conspicuous because of my appearance, I realized that I was among many others in the same predicament.

Sergeant Weide was a confident, surprisingly young woman of average height and build. She had a fair complexion and blonde hair. I noticed that all of the policewomen wore casual slacks and blouses and almost no jewelry. Their only accessory was a gun, held in a holster at the side of their belts. Everyone in the department had an identification badge clipped to his or her clothing.

Throughout my ordeal, I remember appreciating the professionalism of the Detroit Police. I was always treated with respect and kindness. When I gave my victim statement, they were patient with me and sympathetic concerning my emotional behavior.

I gave the full details of the previous twelve hours' events to the police without doubt nor hesitation. My objective at this point was very clear. After what I had just been through, I absolutely would not allow another person to endure the horrific abuse that I had just experienced.

Even though I felt completely destroyed inside, I was determined to summon the strength to co-operate fully with the police.

⁓

Sergeant Weide phoned my sister Zorka shortly after noon to inform her of the assault. Weide gave her directions to the police station and instructed her to bring some clothes for me.

Earlier that day, Zorka had suspected something might be wrong when the Top Hat called wondering why I had not shown up for work. She decided to check up on me so she let herself into my apartment with her key. After checking thoroughly all around, she concluded that everything appeared normal. Since I was not there and my car was gone, she assumed that I was on my way to work.

When Zorka heard from Sergeant Weide she was stunned, even before she learned of the magnitude of the assault. My brother-in-law Jim was at work so she immediately called our parents. My mother baby-sat my niece while my sister and father drove to Detroit.

While I waited for my family at the police department I longed for anything familiar. I wanted to sleep in my own bed, feel the comfort of my own apartment and, most of all, I wanted to soak in a nice hot bath.

But before I could go home, it was necessary for me to go to a hospital for a rape analysis and evidence gathering. I informed Sergeant Weide that I was very anxious to leave Detroit and that I preferred to be examined at a Canadian hospital.

Upon seeing my father and sister when they arrived at the police station, I became emotionally unglued and I sobbed with sadness and guilt. Then, when they were informed of the details of the assault and I saw the looks on their faces, I felt hugely responsible for their reactions.

My father, who did not completely understand English, repeatedly asked for clarification. When he realized the horrible truth, he turned away from everyone and began to cry silently.

Zorka was calm and spoke to me in reassuring tones. She gave me a big hug and said in a soothing voice that everything would be okay. I just wanted to go home.

While I changed my clothes, Sergeant Weide gave instructions to my sister. Two Windsor police officers would meet us at Hotel Dieu Hospital in downtown Windsor to witness the doctor's examination. Since I had no identification, a letter was prepared for Canada Customs, briefly explaining the circumstances and asking them to allow me back across the border into Windsor.

The Examination

As we entered Hotel Dieu's Emergency Entrance, I imagined that everyone was staring at me and knew what had happened. I was overwhelmed with shame and embarrassment. Zorka spoke to the attending nurse, explaining the need for a rape analysis.

As the nurses prepared for the examination, the Windsor Police arrived and spoke quietly with my sister while I sat and waited. Apparently the doctors on duty chose not to examine me, knowing that it would entail future court appearances. They had busy schedules and were not willing to commit the time required to carry out proper procedures for rape cases. I would be kept waiting until a qualified doctor volunteered.

Hours passed when finally, an older man, Dr. Jovanovic, arrived to complete the necessary examination. I dressed in a hospital gown, and with the nurse and two Windsor policemen, (whose names I later learned were Dave Stannard and Mike Kelly), we began the examination. It started with a police photographer taking pictures of the marks and bruises on my face, neck, chest, arms, stomach, and thighs.

With my feet in the stirrups, the doctor gave me a pelvic examination. He dictated his findings into a tape recorder, loudly enough for the policemen to hear and witness.

I remembered the doctor saying that my vagina was torn in several places and that the heavy bleeding was the result of damage to my uterine walls. Samples were taken from underneath my fingernails and loose pubic hairs were collected.

Dr. Jovanovic was extremely gentle but I still struggled to hold back tears of humiliation and pain. I was given the option of taking a "morning-after pill" to prevent pregnancy. In 1976, the drug was considered experimental and was not completely devoid of side affects. The doctor explained that the damage to my uterus, combined with taking the drug, might render me unable to have children. I chose to take the drug. I could absolutely not handle a pregnancy as a result of being raped.

⌒

My distraught father went home and I found my brother-in-law Jim waiting with Zorka when the examination was finished. Feeling utterly embarrassed, I couldn't even look him in the eye. He seemed deeply concerned and relieved when he saw me. I considered him a great guy and a close friend, and I truly appreciated his being there.

When we finally arrived home, I promised my sister that after a nice relaxing bath, I would go next door to her place where my parents and brothers were waiting to see me.

I cannot adequately describe how I felt when I closed my apartment door behind me. It was a mixture of relief, pain and exhaustion. I was finally in my space, my home, and my comfort zone. I immediately ran a hot bath and slid into the water. I couldn't wait to scrub away the memories of my assailants.

The soap scum was so thick from all the scrubbing that I needed to empty the tub and begin again. As the water drained, so did some of the residue of this nightmare. In the bathtub of fresh water, I was able to soak and relax a little.

After my bath I prepared to go next door. I pulled my hair into a tight ponytail and found my loosest-fitting clothes to wear. My face was red and swollen and I didn't bother putting on any make-up. I actually wanted to remain alone and was reluctant to leave my apartment, but my family needed assurances that I was all right.

At my sister's house the mood was very somber. Facing my family was difficult and I kept my head down most of the time. My mother had been crying but was showing me her strong side. She insisted that I return to their home to stay for safety reasons and because she thought that I shouldn't be alone.

Reluctantly, I agreed.

The Aftermath

News of the rape spread quickly among my friends and co-workers. I was unprepared to see anyone, but two of my closest friends from work visited me at my parents' home the next day.

I simply could not shake the extreme feeling of humiliation. Although common sense told me that it wasn't my fault, I felt completely responsible.

Why did I go to Detroit? Why was I driving alone? Why did I have to dress so flashy? Why me? Why? Why? Why?

I needed to be alone. Every time I saw the concern on my mother's face, I felt guilty. My father went to the Serbian priest and began counseling to help him cope with the shame. I wanted to run away and pretend that nothing had happened.

The weekend passed quickly and I gratefully returned to the privacy of my little apartment. Sergeant Weide contacted my sister and made arrangements for me to return to the Detroit Police Station on Monday, February 16th. The Detroit Police had worked around the clock gathering evidence and they already had eight suspects in custody. Using the descriptive information I had given them, they were able to locate Dell's house. Leads gradually exposed the gang and its members.

I was given the task of identifying my assailants in line-ups. First we visited the juvenile facility. As I looked through a small square window, I was surprised to see eight young black boys standing in a row.

Sergeant Weide asked me if I recognized anyone and I replied that yes, the man I knew as Bernard was present. She kept telling me to look and to be sure. I was sure.

Later she informed me that another one of the suspects was also in the line-up and I explained that I didn't realize that there could be more than one at a time. I vowed to be more prepared at the adult jail.

The youth who I was not able to identify would later plead guilty and negotiate a deal with the District Attorney. He testified at the criminal trial as a witness for the prosecution. I was able to successfully identify Joe, Dell, and Melvin, but when I saw Mark in the line-up, I asked the police officer to instruct him to take off his coat.

He looked so feeble and sickly that my response was, "No, that can't be him; he certainly didn't move like that."

Later I learned that it was Mark, but he looked so different because he was on a huge drug downer and was experiencing major withdrawal symptoms.

Seeing these men again took its toll on me. I felt extremely anxious and I was mentally exhausted, but I had to carry on.

The next step was to prepare the evidence for the preliminary hearing. The District Attorney would appear before a judge and present the case against the defendants. They would be represented by council and the judge would determine whether there was enough evidence to send the case to a jury trial.

The judge passed a motion and Bernard, then 16 years old, would be tried as an adult along with the other men.

Testifying

The preliminary hearing was scheduled for February 26th, fourteen days after the rape. I traveled to Detroit several more times after the initial line-ups to help build the case against my assailants. Because I had suppressed some of the details about what had happened to me, some particulars did not arise during the original interrogation. It was the police who told me about the shots that were fired that night.

Several months later, a horrible nightmare woke me up and jolted my memory of the shooting.

I arrived early at the courthouse to meet with the prosecuting attorney, Tom McGuire, who briefly explained what I could expect at the preliminary hearing. I was considered a witness for the State of Michigan and would remain secluded in a witness room until it was my turn to testify.

"When you are on the stand I will direct you with my questions. Tell the truth. If you forget or are not sure of something, don't be afraid to admit it. Do not answer any question impulsively; hesitate briefly before you answer, just in case I have an objection for the court," instructed Mr. McGuire.

He also explained to me that I could not answer a question with, "He raped me." Rape was a conclusion that had yet to be proven, so the appropriate response should be, "He put his penis in my vagina."

I informed Mr. McGuire that, "He put his penis in my vagina," in no way expressed the violence that took place, nor did it describe their vicious aggression against me. I was also told that four of the accused men would be in the courtroom, each with a separate lawyer. Clever Joe would not be among them because he was being held pending a psychiatric examination.

⌒

While waiting in the witness room for the hearing to begin, I had the privilege of seeing Freddy Bennett again, the man I thought of as my Good Samaritan. I was surprised to see him when he entered the room accompanied by his wife and young son. My eyes immediately welled with tears and I felt an enormous weight in my heart. I felt responsible for involving him in this unfortunate situation. Freddy was a decent family man who, by stopping to change the tire for me, was forced into an unwelcome turn of events.

I stood up to greet him. I took his hand and looked directly into his eyes and said softly, "Thank you." Then I turned to his wife, trying really hard not to cry, and repeated, "Thank you."

At that moment the bailiff opened the door and said to me, "We are ready for you."

I entered the courtroom through a side door that led directly to the witness chair. Before sitting, I put my hand on the Bible and I swore to tell the truth. I sat facing an overflowing room of spectators, reporters, and less than ten feet away sat four of the men who had raped me.

As I glanced around the room I realized that, aside from the prosecutor, one defense lawyer, and my sister and her husband, everyone in the room was black. The judge, the security guards, the court reporter, the spectators – they were all black. I felt awkward and out of place.

During my two-hour testimony and cross-examination, I cried while being drilled by each of the four defense attorneys. "Did you fight this time?" "Did you say no that time?" "How do you know which man did what?" And on and on.

My response to these questions would result in sneers and negative comments from the spectators. The judge called for order in the court several times. I repeated my answer, "I had a gun at my head! I did what I was told," again and again.

Michigan had just passed a law that prohibited anyone from bringing a victim's past into evidence, including the fact that I was a virgin before the rape. Testimony was to be specifically about the facts of the case, so during the cross-examination each lawyer attempted to discredit me by trying to make it appear as though the rapes were actually consensual sex.

"But I had a gun pointed at my head. I did what I was told." I stood my ground and articulated the facts. To my surprise, I remembered everything.

In the newspaper the next day, Judge James Del Rio was quoted referring to the case as *"One of the worst cases I've ever heard,"* and, *"[an] animal-like rape,"* (*Windsor Star*, February 27, 1976). That day the judge ordered Dell, Frank, Melvin, and Mark bound over for trial on a total of twelve charges of criminal sexual assault in the first degree (rape) and four counts of kidnapping.

Five months later, Mark, Frank and Bernard pleaded guilty to rape after the prosecutor offered to drop the kidnapping charge in return for a guilty plea to rape. Both carried a life sentence and a minimum of ten years in prison before becoming eligible for parole.

Mark received life imprisonment while Bernard received 10-30 years and Frank received 15-40 years. Dell and Melvin pleaded not guilty and were held in jail until their trial was set at a later date.

Addicted

Shortly after the preliminary hearing, I visited my family doctor and told him the whole story. I complained about tremendous anxiety and repeated nightmares. He prescribed Valium to calm my nerves and he recommended that I see a psychiatrist for counseling.

Contrary to the advice of my closest friends that I should resume my normal routine, I was unable to return to work. I couldn't face people. Whenever I was out in public I felt like everyone was staring and pointing at me.

Valium soon became my friend. It helped numb the pain and distracted me from thinking about my life. A few weeks later I began to suffer from severe headaches. I simply could not cope with the reality of what had happened to me. I lost faith in God and hope for my future.

The psychiatrist I was seeing was concerned only with symptoms and instead of helping me deal with my problems, he prescribed more drugs. I went from not being able to sleep, to wanting to sleep all the time.

I was also depressed and often had suicidal thoughts.

After nine days of suffering from a persistent and severe headache, I drove to the hospital emergency, where the attending physician administered an injection of drugs to ease the pain. They did blood tests which indicated that nothing was seriously wrong, so the doctor concluded that my high levels of anxiety and extreme emotional behavior were psychological.

Even though he didn't know my history, he recommended that I visit my family doctor for a referral to see a different psychiatrist. He prescribed a strong painkiller for the headaches and sent me home.

For several days after the hospital visit, I was sailing with the help of the painkiller drugs. I felt great for the first time in months but the pain relief was short-lived, so I doubled up on the dosage.

My family doctor prescribed unlimited refills, giving me easy access to more and more drugs. When the headache pain resurfaced I discovered that the combination of Valium and painkillers, when taken together, produced a relaxing buzz.

Due to my routine visits to see him, my pharmacist had gotten to know me well; he and I were on a first name basis. One day while I was waiting for a refill, he called my doctor to inform him that he suspected that I was abusing the prescribed drug.

The pharmacist called to me from his back room,

"Your doctor is on the phone. He wants to talk to you."

"Melissa, what the hell are you doing?" he yelled.

"Those drugs are addictive and with the dosages you're taking, they could be lethal! You're smarter than that!"

I was stunned, 'I'm a drug addict!' I thought.

I had always been proud of the fact that I had never smoked or taken drugs, but now I realized what had happened to me was a legal form of addiction. When I returned home, I emptied my pill containers into the toilet and flushed away all indications that I had succumbed to such weakness. What followed were endless days of withdrawal symptoms, including chills, uncontrollable shaking, nausea, and of course, even more severe migraine headaches.

I didn't know what gave me the strength to continue abstaining from this addiction, other than my firm belief that drug users were losers. The headaches eventually subsided, but they occasionally reappeared during stressful stages throughout my life.

Without the drugs it was difficult to return to the unbearable pain of being alone with my thoughts and memories. I truly did not know how to help myself. I would often visit my sister Zorka next door and lament about my problems. I would cry and complain and whine, "Why me? Why me?" I was drowning in self-pity. I was getting nowhere and unable to see a light at the end of the tunnel.

One day Zorka took a risk and confronted me. "How can you keep coming here day after day crying and complaining! This whole ordeal has affected our entire family. I'm hurting too. You can't see it because you're so wrapped up in self pity. I'm getting tired of hearing this over and over again! Why don't you try to do something with your life? You're alive Melissa! You didn't die – so pull yourself together and start *living*!"

I was flabbergasted and couldn't believe what I was hearing. My sister – my best friend – had turned against me! I went back to my apartment and cried for two solid days. Her words rang in my ears and I was so angry I wanted to lash out at her. In time, the anger diminished and I realized that if the words had been spoken by anyone other than Zorka, my response would have been, "Screw you," and my self-indulgent pity would have continued.

I loved and respected my sister and I knew that she felt the same way about me; therefore, I had to take the time to listen and to reflect on my behavior. In the end, I knew Zorka was right. I had to learn to deal with the emotional pain and the headaches. I had to learn to live as normal a life as possible, not only for my sake, but also for the sake of everyone connected to me.

After a few days, I apologized to my sister and brother-in-law and promised to turn my life in a positive direction. It was at this time that my brother-in-law Jim presented me with a gift, my first self-help book: *Your Erroneous Zones* by Dr. Wayne Dyer.

Restored Faith

It is amazing how good things come your way when you make a decision to take charge of your life.

Judy Diebolt, a staff writer for the Detroit Free Press, had written a touching and emotional story about me entitled, *"Rape Victim's Story: Respect, Privacy, Dignity Gone,"* (March 21, 1976). In the article Judy explained that my decision to prosecute was very courageous and one that not many women would make:

"Prosecutors and police officers often have difficulty getting rape victims to testify against their assailants. Many victims feel that going through a trial is like living the nightmare over again. The publicity and the harsh questioning done by defense attorneys often make them feel it simply isn't worth it."

She also wrote: "The particular brutality and gruesomeness of this incident has so outraged the public that the Detroit City Council is trying to bolster freeway patrols."

With Judy's constant involvement in the case we had the opportunity to become friends. It was Judy who informed me about a group of Detroit businessmen who were organizing a trust fund to assist me financially. They wanted to help me pull my life together and start all over again. With the understanding that I was physically and emotionally unable to work, the group of businessmen offered their services for career counseling and their influence to help me find another job in Windsor.

A prominent black Detroit businessman, who had written letters to other executives soliciting money and help, led the efforts for aid. He also organized a special collection to be taken at the Sunday service at Bethel AME Church in Detroit. Judy explained that my benefactor was terribly saddened when he learned that I was white and that my assailants were all black, especially since racial tensions were high in the Detroit area at that time.

When I learned of their concern and read the letters I had received from these caring men, I began to cry and my heart opened a little more.

⌒

A trust fund was organized by the National Bank of Detroit on my behalf. I was to be introduced to the executor, Doris Dedeckre, who would make the disbursements as needed for my living expenses. Judy arranged for Mr. Lewis, Doris and I to meet for lunch, which forced me to leave the seclusion of my apartment.

Doris was a tall, statuesque blonde woman with a classic air of confidence. She wore an expensive conservative suit and was impeccably groomed. I learned that Doris was actually a public relations executive who worked for the businessman who organized the trust fund. She eventually asked if I would be receptive to meeting her employer, Mr. Walton Lewis. She explained that Mr. Lewis was concerned about my reaction to meeting a black man, considering my recent ordeal.

Mr. Lewis had experienced a lifetime of racism and was sensitive to, yet proud of his heritage. I became intrigued by Doris's stories of Mr. Lewis and his struggles. I was fascinated by how he had worked so hard to acquire success in his life and business.

I looked forward to thanking my benefactor personally. What I didn't realize at the time was that meeting Mr. Lewis would change my attitude about the goodness of people.

The three of us met at a restaurant in downtown Windsor. I felt nervous sitting next to Mr. Lewis, not because he was black, but because he was such an important person. He was a big man of average height, slightly balding, and I wasn't sure of his age. I knew he was a grandfather, so I assumed that he was in his sixties.

I was hypnotized by him. There seemed to be an aura outlining his body, yet he seemed humble and unpretentious. My eyes were glued to his face.

He must have felt a bit uncomfortable with me staring at him because he asked if anything was wrong. I answered in astonishment: "You have blue eyes."

I had never imagined a black man having blue eyes. He smiled with genuine amusement and the ice was broken between us.

Mr. Lewis had a profound impact on me because of his commitment and dedication to helping young people finance their education. He was also a prominent member of the religious and cultural community and being involved in the political scene in Detroit. I was honored that he had taken the time to meet me and to make sure that I was going to be okay, considering what had happened to me.

Back to Work

In July 1976, Clever Joe pleaded guilty to kidnapping, first-degree sexual assault, and armed robbery. The psychiatric reports indicated that he was a heavy user of hallucinogenic drugs and described him as "a borderline psychotic who is utterly egocentric and feels no empathy or love for another human being."

The report also added that he had been a heavy drinker since age twelve and called him "anti-social, manipulative and criminally motivated." (*Detroit Free Press*, March 31, 1985). In addition the report added that Clever Joe referred to "his omnipresent powers as Satan." (*Windsor Star*, July 30, 1976). He was sentenced to two terms of life imprisonment.

Mark, Frank, Bernard, Joe and the juvenile pleaded guilty and had begun serving their sentences; Melvin and Dell pleaded not guilty and were scheduled to go on trial October 11, 1976.

The efficiency of the Detroit Police Department and the efforts of the District Attorney's office ensured a speedy trial. I only had to wait eight months, whereas it typically took years to begin a trial.

In the interim, I pro-actively worked at restoring some normalcy into my life. I benefited greatly from reading my first self-help book, *Your Erroneous Zones*, so I decided that the local library would be an obvious starting point.

I searched endlessly for any book that could help me identify my thoughts and feelings pertaining to sexual assault, but I was unsuccessful. However, I did find a book with references to statistics concerning rape victims. I learned that there were two common life-changing results that many victims were unable to overcome:

1) Rape victims, after their attacks, could not have a normal sex life or enjoy sexual relations;
2) Rape victims lived with some degree of fear for the rest of their lives.

It was at this time that I made a decisive goal to overcome the obstacles I had researched, and to not live my life as a *statistic*. I had made a promise to my sister and now I was making one to myself. I would be strong and take control of my life.

⌒

My first order of business was to find a job. With the help of Mr. Lewis and his friends at the National Bank of Detroit, letters of introduction were sent to the major banks in the Windsor area, asking that my application be considered for any job openings.

Within weeks, I was called for an interview with the Canadian Imperial Bank of Commerce. I dressed in business attire and I felt confident during the interview with the assistant manager at the bank, until he asked me about my relationship with the writer of the recommendation letter. I interpreted the question as inappropriate and thought that he was assuming that the letter's author and I were in an illicit relationship.

With a serious and firm voice I answered, "I was the woman who was kidnapped and raped after getting a flat tire on the freeway in Detroit and these people are just trying to help me." I could see his stunned reaction to my confession, but I was also stunned at myself for being so abrupt and impulsive.

The interview was over and as I exited the bank, I held my head proudly in an attempt to disguise my true feelings of insecurity and helplessness.

When I returned home, I threw myself on my bed and cried. My efforts to put myself out in the world were humiliating.

When I found myself unable to cope with situations, I would try to sleep, hoping that when I awakened the intrusive feelings and emotions would become less intense, or better yet, disappear.

That afternoon I awoke with a start to the sound of the phone ringing. It was a call from the bank offering me an entry-level position. Perhaps now I could begin a new phase of my life with this new job.

I settled comfortably into my new position and immediately developed close friendships with several of my co-workers.

I was soon promoted to bank teller, which allowed me to interact with customers and business clients. I enjoyed being in the midst of what seemed to be the center of Windsor's business community. I especially loved counting money and monitoring the accounts of my favorite customers, hoping to learn some of their success secrets. Being in the professional banking atmosphere re-awakened some of the ambition I had possessed before the rape. I considered this a major improvement in my overall outlook on life and the future.

Unfortunately, recurring nightmares, migraine headaches, and fits of anxiety caused me to call in sick quite often, which only added to my feelings of guilt. Even though most of my co-workers seemed to know about my ordeal, I felt as if I was letting them down and disappointing my superiors. I decided that I needed to take charge of improving my life, so my next step was to find a new therapist.

Since I was no longer taking prescribed drugs, I was not seeing a psychiatrist. So I asked my family doctor to refer me to a psychologist or a social worker. I explained that I wanted to go some place where the atmosphere would be therapeutic rather than clinical and sterile. He referred me to his brother, Dr. Bob, a psychologist with a private practice.

A Different Twist

Dr. Bob (who preferred to be called by his first name) had a basement office in an old house on Ouellette Avenue, Windsor's main street. His office didn't strike me as typical. It was cluttered, a little messy, and very casual, yet it seemed comfortable enough.

When I saw Dr. Bob for the first time in the fall of 1976, he was entirely different from what I had expected. He had large, brown eyes, a baby face, dark complexion, and dark, curly hair. He was about five feet, ten inches tall with a small build. He wore casual jeans and a wrinkled gray sweater that looked as though he had slept in it. He had a charming smile and personality and I was immediately attracted to him.

I later discovered that he was thirty-seven years old, but to me he looked much younger.

Our first session went well because our personalities clicked. I felt comfortable with Dr. Bob and free to talk to him about anything. On my way home afterwards, I felt satisfied that I would finally get the professional help that I so desperately needed.

I saw Dr. Bob twice a week for three more weeks. I had taken to calling him just "Bob" as I felt so comfortable with him. During our last session he announced that I no longer needed therapy since I was a smart, articulate person and that regardless of the immense trauma that I had suffered, I was well on my way to a healthy future.

On the other hand, I felt that I was being totally abandoned by this declaration. Even though there was an obvious improvement in my outlook and the recovery process was on its way, I could hardly imagine being cured of the demons that haunted me daily. I still had constant nightmares. I was still filled with fear and my self-esteem was non-existent. Why was he dismissing our sessions so nonchalantly?

I was confused and frustrated and, I missed talking to him.

Three weeks later I noticed that Dr. Bob had not cashed any of my checks. It gave me a perfect excuse to call him.

"Dr. Bob, it's Melissa. I was just wondering why you haven't cashed my checks. Is there a problem?"

"I can't accept payment from you Melissa. You know how I feel about you; it wouldn't be right."

"What was he talking about?," I wondered.

His explanation for discontinuing our therapy sessions was simple; he had fallen for me. He wanted to start seeing me, to go out on dates and to have a relationship.

I couldn't believe it! A professional man, an educated doctor of psychology was interested in me?

I was so desperate to connect with someone, that without hindsight, I didn't realize that Bob was actually attracted to my naivete and vulnerability.

We started dating and I proudly told my family and friends that I was going out with a doctor. It made me feel very special that someone of his position was interested in me.

Bob frequently took me to public places where people would see us together. After a while, because of the age difference, it seemed like he was taking me places where he could flaunt his very young pretty girlfriend (I was 19 years old to his 37 years). He encouraged me to dress in sexy outfits and he was always very affectionate in public.

One night after an elegant dinner, Bob and I went dancing at a Windsor nightclub. A nurse from his brother's office saw us together and immediately reported to my family doctor that Bob and I were out together. I happened to be at Bob's house the next evening, when my doctor unexpectedly dropped by. Although Bob made every attempt to distract his brother and prevent him from seeing me inside the house, I knew that a confrontation was inevitable.

I could hear my doctor at the door:

"What the hell is the matter with you, Bob? She's a patient of yours! Being with her is completely unethical. You're jeopardizing your career!"

Bob mumbled a response.

I heard his brother reply, "It's not worth it – you're wrong."

It became a heated argument. My doctor was completely disgusted with the entire situation. His brother left and Bob returned to where I was sitting.

He was angry.

"My brother was always the smart one in the family. Everything I do is wrong in his eyes. I've never been able to measure up," he complained.

He dismissed the subject with, "I don't give a shit what he thinks. I'm going to do whatever I want."

As the days went by, I became more and more emotionally dependent on Bob. I expected him to be my savior. It allowed me to avoid the work I needed to do for me to become more mature and responsible on my own.

When the time came for us to become more intimate, in our attempts do to so, the unthinkable happened.

Bob could not get an erection.

He blamed me, and of course, I blamed myself.

I assumed that because of the rape, he viewed me as a scarred woman and therefore did not find me sexually attractive.

Or, perhaps he was feeling guilty about being with a former patient.

In actuality, his inability to consummate our relationship had nothing to do with me.

Bob had shown signs of being more of a mess emotionally than I was. Whenever I had made any attempts to be physically close to him, such as to hug him or touch him, he would resort to name-calling. He constantly accused me of being neurotic, emotionally unstable, and sick.

When he was angry, he called me "the fucking nutcase."

My only reaction to these horrible remarks was to cry.

Yes, I was emotionally unstable and perhaps even neurotic, but why was Bob doing this to me?

One evening, Bob and I talked seriously about his inability to consummate our relationship. For the first time I became suspicious that this problem was not something new.

I asked him outright, "Bob, are you gay?"

He became frustrated and responded, "I've been with women before."

That night we decided to go on a week's vacation to the Bahamas. We hoped that the relaxation and sunny weather would help create a romantic setting for us.

The trip proved to be a total disaster!

Although we slept in the same bed, Bob did not touch me once. During the entire vacation he gawked at and commented on the "tomatoes" at the beach, which was how he referred to beautiful women.

I felt more and more unattractive and undesirable. I became depressed and began to withdraw.

When we returned home, something extraordinary happened. Bob called me to tell me about a recent conversation with a female friend. The subject of my rape came up and he claimed that she told him that "being raped by black men was actually a sexual fantasy for most white women."

Bob implied that the inner turmoil, and the guilt and shame that I was experiencing was exaggerated, if not entirely false. I was merely putting on a "poor victim" act.

I went completely crazy at his ludicrous suggestion!!

I screamed back at him "You have no fucking idea what you're talking about! I may not be a fucking doctor but I know that rape has nothing to do with sex! It's about power and violence and control. So you'd better get your head examined because it's *you* who needs help if you believe that bullshit!"

I hung up. I felt like I had been raped again. Fortunately, thanks to the Detroit Police Department, I had learned that rape was not a sexual act, but an act of violence. Otherwise, I would probably never have understood the extent to which Bob was manipulating me.

We were through!

Shortly after this incident, Bob took a leave from his private practice and went to Europe for six months.

After much reflection on the subject, I recognized that Bob was using his professional background as a weapon to control me and to make *himself* feel significant. He had found someone weaker than himself and he was taking advantage of the situation.

Years later, I bumped into him at an elevator we were both about to ride, and he casually turned to me and said, "I'll wait for the next one."

As the years went by it became apparent that I had been emotionally and mentally abused in this sick relationship. It was too late to bring forth a lawsuit, but I did file a complaint with the Ontario Psychological Association.

Back to Business

After this unexpected emotional setback from someone who was supposed to be helping me, I became more determined to improve my life. Even though I felt betrayed and disappointed, I was also tired of constantly being a pawn in someone else's game. I now understood that the world was full of quacks and that there would always be adversity and negativity to contend with.

This point was confirmed for me when Doris Dedeckre disclosed that along with the good wishes and donations for the trust fund, there was hate mail too. Naturally these letters were destroyed and I didn't get to read them, but it was hard to believe that people could be so angry and cruel.

I knew that I had done what I had to do to save my life.

The public was trying to turn my case into a racial issue and was accusing the police of giving me special treatment because I was white.

What people didn't realize was, the fact that my assailants were black was of no relevance to me. I was totally aware that crime and criminals came in all shapes, sizes and colors.

As far as I was concerned, the Detroit Police handled my case in the most professional and efficient manner possible.

⁓

I was advised to hire a lawyer in order to protect myself as a witness for the State of Michigan. I contacted a prominent Windsor lawyer and asked for his help. He, in turn, referred a colleague of his from Detroit who agreed to represent me. His name was Mark Weiss and we agreed to meet at the Top Hat.

When I first saw Mark, I had to smile in amusement because it took a great deal of confidence to dress the way he did. Mark was wearing a yellow striped seersucker suit and bow tie. He was a dead ringer for Steve Guttenberg, the actor. He was quite young and very cute! He was twenty-seven years old, only eight years my senior, and after talking to him about my ordeal, I was relieved that I didn't have to deal with a stuffy, older man.

Mark was available to answer any questions or concerns that developed before the trial and I was grateful to have someone like him to relate to.

The Trial

Several months later Sergeant Weide finally called to inform me of the trial date set for October, 1976, and the likelihood that my testimony would last a couple of days. She also mentioned that Melvin, during his incarceration pending the outcome of the trial, had been assaulted and beaten by some of his fellow inmates.

Apparently, a rapist is considered the lowest of the low in prison because rape victims are usually women and children. Sergeant Weide assured me that this type of beating was common, and she wanted me to be prepared for when I saw Melvin in the courtroom.

When I did, I felt responsible for what had happened to him.

I noticed that I blamed myself for so many things and shame and guilt were constantly in the back of my mind.

By experiencing the final hurdle of the trial, I looked forward to finishing that chapter of my life and moving on.

Regardless of the outcome, I felt justified that I had done my part by getting these men off the street. On October 19, 1976, I testified against Melvin, then 19, and Dell, then 23, before a jury of seven men and five women. Dell waived his right to a jury trial and so the trial judge, Judge Susan Borman, would render his verdict.

My testimony lasted one and a half days and I was very happy for it to finally be over. The trial lasted for another two weeks and I followed the details in the newspaper. Melvin denied that he had ever raped me and he claimed that he actually tried to rescue me from the other men.

"I couldn't do nothing about it. I had no gun." he testified.

He said that he went to a friend's house several doors away and told two female friends what was happening.

Both women testified in court, corroborating the story of his visit. Joe testified in Dell and Melvin's defense that they had no idea that I was kidnapped.

On the other hand, I had positively identified him as one of the most vicious of my assailants and had picked him out of a line-up. I definitely remembered him being on top of me because he had been wearing my medallion choker around his neck that night. Also, Melvin was the one who I saw driving my Pacer after I was kidnapped on the highway.

I felt disheartened when I heard that the jury took forty-two hours to render a verdict. The prosecutor, Tom McGuire, was quoted as saying, "I thought it was the strongest case I had ever tried" (*Detroit News*, November 11, 1976).

Melvin was found guilty of one count of kidnapping and

armed robbery, and two counts of sexual assault and was sentenced to life in prison.

Dell's defense was that he had no idea I was at his home against my will, nor was he told by Joe or by me that I had been kidnapped. Other testimony from police and medical witnesses indicated that my face was badly beaten and my overall appearance was in complete disarray. I reminded the jury that my four-inch heel was missing from one of my boots and that it was obvious that I was struggling to walk in them.

On November 15, 1976, Dell was found not guilty of sexual assault and Judge Borman, in her statement, said that she could not absolutely, without a reasonable doubt know whether Dell was aware that my presence at his home was involuntary.

Sergeant Weide called me with the verdict before it hit the papers, and I honestly was relieved that Dell was acquitted. I didn't consider him a violent man and during the trial it was revealed that he was gay. Coming out before his friends was enough of a price to pay. Several months later I learned that he was arrested on drug charges and ended up in prison anyway.

Now that the trial was over and my assailants were imprisoned, I should have felt relieved but I didn't. I had serious doubts that I would ever feel normal again.

The Settlement

Within a year of the completion of the criminal trial my attorney, Mark Weiss, filed a personal injury lawsuit against the City of Detroit and Wayne County, Michigan, on my behalf. The lawsuit charged that they were negligent in their duties to provide adequate protection on the freeway on the night of February 12, 1976.

My abduction and subsequent gang rape had so outraged the public that William G. Milliken, then governor, ordered State Police to patrol Detroit freeways, (which they still do). The City of Detroit had reduced its patrols because of layoffs and budget cuts.

Knowing it would take years for the legal system to decide the outcome of the lawsuit, I continued the struggle to live a normal life. Mark kept in regular contact updating me with details of the progress of the case.

Finally, in April of 1983, seven years after the crime, an out of court settlement was reached with the City of Detroit for $152,000. Mark called me at work to inform me of the offer and he visited the bank that afternoon so that I could sign the agreement.

Early the next morning, Eleanor, my former boss at the bank called me at home to congratulate me on the victory. She informed me that the settlement was the top news story on the Windsor and Detroit radio stations. I was horrified for I had barely absorbed the news myself.

When I arrived at the bank, my friend and co-worker, Kathleen, asked me to meet her in the ladies' room. She notified me that the entire staff was talking about my recent windfall. She felt it necessary to prepare me for an onslaught of gossip within our workplace. I was completely unprepared for the unexpected attention.

⌒

I later learned that it was Mark who had leaked the story to the press and when I questioned him about it, he answered, "The settlement is a matter of public record. Besides, the publicity will help with our pending lawsuit against Wayne County."

After paying seven years of legal expenses and the attorney's contingency fee, the settlement was considerably less than the original $152,000. I had enough money to pay off the small mortgage on my two-bedroom bungalow, which I had purchased a few years earlier, buy a new car and spend a week in Florida. The remainder of the funds was shared with my family. In no time at all, the money was gone.

I experienced some guilty feelings because of the money and

it was necessary for me, through counseling, to understand its symbolic significance. Rather than viewing the settlement as "dirty money," I was encouraged to accept it as income earned and deserved.

Still pending was the lawsuit against Wayne County, Michigan.

Disappointment

As the civil case against Wayne County progressed, Mark explained that we had won our right to sue four times in the Court of Appeals. The County's attempt to have it heard at the Supreme Court level was denied. Per my instructions, Mark was aggressively trying to negotiate an out of court settlement to save me from the trauma of another trial. Richard Kudla, the lawyer for Wayne County, refused to consider any type of settlement.

As time passed, I became more and more anxious, for I knew that the trial would expose my entire personal life. For the jury's sake, it would be necessary to recount the horrible details of my abduction and gang rape, as well as reveal the status of my current and past relationships, work experience and general lifestyle.

As jury selection began in June of 1985, I became so stressed that I doubted my ability to summon the strength I had built over the years.

What actually transpired during the three-week trial

was a farce. Although my attorney had proven himself to be an excellent negotiator, he lacked experience in the actual courtroom. Richard Kudla, Wayne County's lawyer, was loud, abrasive and cocky. The courtroom was his stage and he was the star of the show.

On the other hand, Mark was obsessed about how he looked and how I was dressed.

"We have to make a good impression on the jury," he said.

The highlight of the trial was the testimony of William Lucas, then County Sheriff. He was a high profile official with political aspirations, who appeared in the courtroom with his entourage of body guards and assistants. He also attracted the news media that followed him constantly. He looked so handsome in his expensive suit that everyone, myself included, was star struck.

During Lucas' testimony he maintained that it was not his responsibility to patrol Detroit freeways. He presented himself as polished, confident and credible and he was.

In contrast, I found it humiliating to have to justify myself to the jury. I was angry and resentful at having to beg for approval from total strangers.

The drama escalated during closing statements when Kudla pointed at me and declared, "Look at her. She comes to court every day with make-up, her nails manicured, wearing nice clothes. She drives a new car, has a good job, owns her home, is pretty, and successful." He implied that there was no need for a settlement; that I was perfectly fine and how could I even think of any compensation.

The jury of three men and three women rendered a verdict within three hours, in favor of the defendant, Wayne County.

Richard Kudla was actually surprised by his win.

"I can't believe it!" he exclaimed to the press.

Of course, Mark was very upset about our loss. Years of hard work had gone down the drain. The jury had decided that outward appearances were more convincing and justified than the painful struggles that were going on inside.

Although I felt crushed and defeated, I was relieved that it was finally over. Now it was time to put the past behind me and to get on with the rest of my life.

Life in Perspective

I heard Oprah say on her TV show once, "You can line up any ten people and they will all have a story."

Even though I understand life is a challenge for everyone, I know I will never get over what happened to me that night.

Over the years I have forced myself to conquer the horrible memories that often intruded into my daily routine.

Almost thirty years later I still experience nightmares, restless sleep patterns, and severe headaches during stressful times, but I have learned to accept these aberrations as part of my everyday life. I also struggle with a weight problem and I use food as a coping mechanism.

Today the question that I am most asked is, "How could you possibly enjoy sex after what happened to you?"

My answer is:

"Rape is about violence, control and power. Sex is the weapon, but rape is not sex. Sex should be about love, commitment and consent; sex and rape are completely opposite from each other."

I found this concept easy to comprehend and I had no trouble separating the two in my life.

Unfortunately, there is still a huge stigma associated with rape victims today. Unlike some women who have been violated, I learned to accept what happened to me and to challenge the inner feelings of shame and embarrassment that accompanied it.

In my case, I was able to overcome the stigma by talking about it openly. I talked to my sister, my friends, and even strangers, who questioned me unexpectedly. I talked with counsellors, therapists and reporters. I read every newspaper article available pertaining to rape and watched every talk show that addressed the topic.

Knowledge is power and the more I learned, the better I felt about myself.

I am neither shy nor embarrassed to speak of my ordeal and I have come to terms with the direction of my life.

My friends joke about my owning every self-help book on the market. I laugh too, especially when I attempt to organize the two hundred or more books that I own.

I particularly enjoy biographies because I love to learn from other people's experiences. When I feel down or depressed, I get inspiration from my favourite spiritual or self-help book.

I believe everything in life has a positive side and although I was the victim of a horrible circumstance, it probably made me a better person than I otherwise would have been.

It has motivated me to question life and dig deep for answers. I studied various religions and developed my own philosophy and value system.

This growth process instilled within me the confidence to face the continuous challenges that have come my way.

After eight years in the banking industry, I opened a retail business in 1985 and have operated it successfully for over eighteen years. Being my own boss allowed me the opportunity to continue my education by attending business and marketing seminars. I belong to several business organizations and I volunteer my services in the non-profit sector.

My first marriage produced an extraordinary addition to my life, my first child, a son. After having been told that it was unlikely that I would be able to have children, getting pregnant was an unexpected joy. Although my second marriage also ended in divorce, I was blessed with two beautiful daughters.

Becoming a mother taught me that I wasn't the center of the universe. I learned to expand the focus of my life and I realized the huge and direct impact I had on my children's lives. Having children has given me purpose and greater determination to improve myself.

One of the greatest challenges in my life has been to covercome fear.

After the rape, I was filled with fear.

I was afraid to face people.

I was afraid that I would be scarred and branded for life.

I was afraid that I would never again be accepted as the person I was before the rape.

Conversely, remembering the peaceful feelings that encompassed me during my out-of-body experience during the rape, I do not fear death.

The one thing I wanted was to feel normal and not be pitied for what I had gone through.

As I contemplate the events of my life, it occurs to me that I have come full circle. Although I would have done some things differently, I have no regrets.

There is still much room for improvement but basically, I am content. One of my greatest accomplishments is that I live a normal life and that being brutally raped did not kill my spirit.

Epilogue

Joe, then 22, was sentenced to two terms of life imprisonment.

Dell, then 23, was found not guilty of rape but sentenced to prison on other unrelated charges.

Frank (Spoon), then 18, was sentenced to 15-40 years in prison; he was paroled in August 1983.

Bernard, then 16, was sentenced as an adult to 10-30 years. He was paroled in May 1982 and finished his parole in May 1984.

James, then 15 and under the authority of the juvenile court in Wayne County, his file was expunged and could not be located.

Marcus, then 17, was sentenced to life imprisonment.

Melvin, then 19, was sentenced to life imprisonment.

In 1985, Michigan Governor William Milliken provided state police patrols on Detroit area freeways that are still enforced today.

Partly due to my commendation, the Sexual Assault Unit of the Detroit Police Department was presented with an Award of Merit in 1976.

Walton Lewis died in 1995. In 1941, he founded Lewis & Thompson Agency Inc., a Detroit insurance company that was a pioneer in the insurance for black people. He participated in more than two dozen civic and business associations and was one of the first employers to take black youth into the office to help them gain some practical business knowledge.

Dr. Claude Vincent of the University of Windsor died in 1995. After attempting to locate a copy of his textbook about victims of crime at the University of Windsor, I was informed that no such book existed. Apparently, he was unable to publish the book before his death.

My attempts to locate Freddy Bennett, my Good Samaritan, were unsuccessful. I hope he and is family are well.

Shortly after losing the civil suit against Wayne County, Mark Weiss left his law firm and joined one that would give him more trial experience.

After two other complaints were filed about Dr. Bob, he resigned from his position as a pyschologist in 2003 with the understanding that he could no longer practice or offer counseling.

Special Thanks

To Elaine Weeks and Vanda O'Keefe of Walkerville Publishing, for your encouragement and assistance during the process of writing this book.

To Linda Muldoon for your support and always knowing the right thing to say.

To Gloria Kawala, for being a good listener and an encouraging friend.

And, to Mike Hereford for your friendship and knowing you will always be there if I need help.

Help for Victims of Sexual Assault

What to do if you've been sexually assaulted:

If you have been sexually assaulted by a family member, a colleague, a teacher or a stranger, contact the police immediately to file a report. Do not be concerned about the person who has assaulted you. Be concerned for yourself.

If you have delayed contacting the police for various reasons, please know that you can still go to them, even years after the attack, to make a charge.

If you need help coping with the aftermath of sexual assault, please contact your local Sexual Assault Crisis Center. You should find the number in the white pages of your phone book.

You can call the National Sexual Assault Hotline, operated by RAINN, 24 hours a day at **1-800-656-HOPE** (4673), 635-B Pennsylvania Avenue, SE, Washington, D.C. 20003 **www.rainn.org.**

All local U.S. rape crisis hotlines will be listed on the rain. org website.

You'll also be able to narrow your search if you are looking for specialized services – groups for male, elderly, teen or disabled survivors, programs for people under age 12, spouses or family members, adults molested as children or GLBT survivors, as well as services via TTY, in Spanish or other languages.

A good source of information and support to survivors on the internet and serves nearly 1 million hits yearly through its page and message views in the chat rooms, forums and of course, the main site itself @

www.hopeforhealing.org

Detroit Sexual Assault Crisis Center
Rape Counseling Center
Detroit Police Dept.
4201 St. Antoine
Detroit MI 48201
313-833-1660

Windsor Sexual Assault Crisis Center
24hr Crisis Line 519-253-9667

Sexual Assault Treatment Center/Safekids
1030 Ouellette Avenue, Windsor, ON
519-255-2334

I remember following the case when it happened. It was the most disgusting crime I had ever imagined. Melissa, I'm so glad you were able to survive to tell the story. Just the fact that you are able to tell it says volumes about your character. It will help many women who have been and will be victims of this terrible type of crime. I wish you the best life a person could have. You are truly an example of the strength possible in a human being. God bless you.
DH

Melissa's book is not only about her kidnapping and gang rape but how she managed to escape and then recover from this traumatic event. The book describes the journey she took to achieve a normal life once again. The message she wants to leave the reader is that it is possible to overcome the various challenges life throws at you, no matter how difficult. Communication is one of the keys – you should not be ashamed or afraid to come forward and tell someone what has happened to you.

Reading The Queen's Daughter is a valuable experience for other victims of sexual assault as they can follow Melissa's thought process while she was in captivity: disbelief that this is happening... thinking she's going to die... wanting to die... disbelief she is still alive... wanting to escape... then deciding how she can bargain for her life. When a victim reads her book they can see how their feelings were similar to Melissa's – that this is a common thread to victims of sexual assault. Seeing how Melissa thought society regarded her after the assault is very worthwhile as well. Reading The Queen's Daughter will help victims in their own recovery process.
Lydia Fiorini, Executive Director,
Windsor Sexual Assault Crisis Centre

This is above all, a story of triumph and I applaud [Melissa's] courage... I'm one of those people who has always believed that all things that happen to us in life, whether good or bad, have a purpose. One can scarcely imagine what purpose your ordeal could have had until perhaps now. We all influence other people's lives in ways that we can only imagine, but I'm sure that with the release of this book, you will influence countless lives in profound and meaningful ways that you probably never would have thought possible even a few years ago. May you continue to enrich your own life along the way.

R & M

A couple of similar victim friends of mine also say that they could not move ahead as persons until they were able to forgive their assailant... a really difficult truth to portray to those victims who are still in the midst of their journey and still so hurt and violated, still filled with anger and a desire for justice based in revenge. We just have to support and nurture them and be patient for their own movement to begin within themselves.

Lou Drouillard
St. Leonard's House Chaplaincy Service

Visit The Queen's Daughter web site:
www.queensdaughter.com

If you have questions,
need help or advice, e-mail
mel@queensdaughter.com

*A portion of the proceeds from this book
will be donated to the Windsor Sexual Assault Crisis Center
and the Detroit Police Department Rape Counseling Center.*

.